I0477861

Transforming Threat Detection and Response

AI IN CYBERSECURITY

Arun Kumar Krishna | CISSP

CTO, Sennovate Inc

AI in Cybersecurity: Transforming Threat Detection and Response

AUTHOR : ARUN KUMAR KRISHNA, CISSP

CTO, SENNOVATE INC

TABLE OF CONTENTS

INTRODUCTION

SCOPE AND STRUCTURE OF THE BOOK

This book provides a comprehensive guide on how AI technologies are revolutionizing cybersecurity. We explore various AI techniques and their applications in threat detection and response. Through real-world case studies, we demonstrate the effectiveness of AI in combating cyber threats. Additionally, we offer implementation strategies to help organizations integrate AI into their existing cybersecurity frameworks. Finally, we look ahead to future trends, highlighting emerging technologies and their potential impact.

WHAT YOU WILL LEARN

- AI Technologies in Cybersecurity: An in-depth look at ML, DL, NLP, and Anomaly Detection, and their roles in enhancing cybersecurity.

- OCR and Visual AI: How these technologies are being used to detect and prevent document-based attacks and monitor visual data for suspicious activities.

- Real-World Case Studies: Success stories and lessons learned from various industries that have implemented AI-driven security solutions.

- Implementation Strategies: Practical steps and best practices for integrating AI into cybersecurity frameworks.

- Future Trends: Emerging AI technologies and predictions for the future of AI in cybersecurity.

THE EVOLUTION OF CYBERSECURITY

EARLY DAYS: REACTIVE MEASURES

In the initial stages of the internet and computing, cybersecurity was relatively straightforward. The primary threats came in the form of basic viruses and worms. During this period, cybersecurity measures were largely reactive. Antivirus software, which was designed to detect and remove known threats, was the cornerstone of security strategies. Firewalls were used to filter traffic between trusted and untrusted networks, providing a basic level of protection against external threats.

RISE OF THE INTERNET: INCREASED CONNECTIVITY AND RISKS

As the internet grew in popularity, the nature of cybersecurity threats began to change. Increased connectivity meant that more systems were exposed to potential attackers. Hackers started to exploit vulnerabilities in software and networks, leading to a rise in more sophisticated forms of cyberattacks such as phishing, malware, and denial-of-service (DoS) attacks. During this period, organizations began to recognize the importance of proactive cybersecurity measures, including regular software updates, vulnerability assessments, and the adoption of intrusion detection systems (IDS).

THE ERA OF E-COMMERCE: PROTECTING DIGITAL TRANSACTIONS

The advent of e-commerce brought new challenges and opportunities for cybersecurity. Protecting online transactions became a critical concern as financial data and personal information were increasingly being exchanged over the internet. Encryption technologies were developed to secure data in transit, and secure socket layer (SSL) certificates became standard for e-commerce websites. Payment card industry data security standards (PCI DSS) were established to ensure the protection of cardholder data.

CLOUD COMPUTING AND MOBILE DEVICES: EXPANDING THE ATTACK SURFACE

The proliferation of cloud computing and mobile devices further expanded the cybersecurity landscape. Organizations began to store sensitive data in cloud environments, and employees increasingly accessed corporate networks through mobile devices. This shift introduced new security challenges, including securing data across multiple environments and managing the risks associated with mobile device usage. Cybersecurity strategies evolved to include cloud security measures, mobile device management (MDM), and endpoint protection solutions.

ADVANCED PERSISTENT THREATS (APTS) AND NATION-STATE ACTORS

In the past decade, the cybersecurity landscape has been dominated by the rise of advanced persistent threats (APTs) and nation-state actors. These sophisticated adversaries use a combination of advanced techniques, including social engineering, zero-day exploits, and custom malware, to achieve their objectives. APTs are characterized by their persistence and the ability to remain undetected within target networks for extended periods. Nation-state actors often have significant resources and capabilities, making them formidable adversaries. In response, organizations have had to adopt more advanced cybersecurity measures, including threat intelligence, behavioral analysis, and advanced endpoint detection and response (EDR) solutions.

THE ROLE OF ARTIFICIAL INTELLIGENCE (AI)

Today, AI is playing a transformative role in cybersecurity. AI technologies, such as machine learning and deep learning, are being used to enhance threat detection and response. AI-driven solutions can analyze vast amounts of data in real-time, identifying patterns and anomalies that may indicate a cyber threat. By automating routine tasks and providing intelligent insights, AI enables security teams to respond more quickly and effectively to threats. Additionally, AI-powered threat intelligence platforms provide organizations with real-time insights into emerging threats and vulnerabilities.

FUTURE TRENDS AND CHALLENGES

As we look to the future, cybersecurity will continue to evolve in response to new technologies and emerging threats. The rise of the Internet of Things (IoT), quantum computing, and 5G networks will introduce new security challenges. Organizations will need to stay ahead of these trends by adopting advanced cybersecurity measures and continuously updating their security strategies. Collaboration and information sharing will also play a crucial role in enhancing global cybersecurity resilience.

THE ROLE OF AI IN CYBERSECURITY

ENHANCED THREAT DETECTION

One of the most significant contributions of AI to cybersecurity is its ability to enhance threat detection capabilities. Traditional cybersecurity measures often rely on signature-based detection methods, which can only identify known threats. AI, on the other hand, leverages machine learning algorithms to analyze large volumes of data and identify patterns and anomalies that may indicate malicious activity. By continuously learning from new data, AI systems can detect previously unknown threats and adapt to evolving attack techniques. This proactive approach allows organizations to stay ahead of cyber attackers and mitigate risks before they cause significant damage.

AUTOMATION OF ROUTINE TASKS

Cybersecurity teams often face an overwhelming number of alerts and incidents that need to be investigated and addressed. AI can automate many of these routine tasks, freeing up valuable time and resources for security professionals to focus on more complex and strategic activities. For example, AI-driven security information and event management (SIEM) systems can automatically correlate and analyze security events from multiple sources, providing real-time insights and prioritizing alerts based on their severity. Additionally, AI-powered security orchestration, automation, and response (SOAR) platforms can automate incident response processes, such as containing threats, applying patches, and updating security policies, significantly reducing response times and improving overall efficiency.

BEHAVIOURAL ANALYSIS AND ANOMALY DETECTION

AI excels at analyzing user behavior and identifying deviations from normal patterns. By establishing a baseline of typical behavior for each user and system, AI can detect anomalies that may indicate a security breach or insider threat. For example, if an employee suddenly starts accessing sensitive files they have never accessed before or logs in from an unusual location, AI can flag this behavior for further investigation. Behavioral analysis is particularly effective in detecting advanced persistent threats (APTs) and other sophisticated attacks that often evade traditional security measures.

PREDICTIVE ANALYTICS

AI's predictive analytics capabilities allow organizations to anticipate potential cyber threats and take proactive measures to prevent them. By analyzing historical data and identifying trends, AI can forecast future attack patterns and vulnerabilities. This enables organizations to prioritize their security efforts and allocate resources more effectively. For example, predictive analytics can help identify which systems or applications are most likely to be targeted based on current threat intelligence, allowing security teams to implement additional safeguards and strengthen defenses in those areas.

ADVANCED THREAT INTELLIGENCE

AI-driven threat intelligence platforms aggregate and analyze data from various sources, including open-source intelligence (OSINT), dark web monitoring, and proprietary threat feeds. By leveraging natural language processing (NLP) and machine learning, these platforms can identify emerging threats, track the activities of cybercriminal groups, and provide actionable insights in real-time. This comprehensive and up-to-date threat intelligence enables organizations to make informed decisions and stay ahead of the latest cyber threats.

FRAUD DETECTION AND PREVENTION

AI plays a crucial role in detecting and preventing fraud, particularly in industries such as finance and e-commerce. Machine learning algorithms can analyze transaction data and identify patterns indicative of fraudulent activity. For example, AI can detect anomalies in credit card transactions, such as unusually high spending or transactions from multiple locations within a short period. By flagging these anomalies in real-time, AI helps prevent fraudulent transactions and minimizes financial losses. Additionally, AI-driven identity verification solutions can enhance security by accurately verifying user identities and detecting fraudulent attempts to create fake accounts or access sensitive information.

ADAPTIVE SECURITY SYSTEMS

AI enables the development of adaptive security systems that can dynamically adjust their defenses based on the evolving threat landscape. These systems use continuous learning and feedback mechanisms to update their models and improve their accuracy over time. For example, an AI-powered intrusion prevention system (IPS) can automatically adjust its rules and signatures based on new threat intelligence and attack patterns. This adaptability ensures that security measures remain effective against emerging threats and reduces the need for manual intervention and updates.

WHY AI IS ESSENTIAL FOR MODERN THREAT DETECTION

HANDLING THE VOLUME AND COMPLEXITY OF DATA

Modern organizations generate and process an enormous amount of data daily. This data includes network traffic, user activities, transaction records, and logs from various applications and devices. Traditional security tools and human analysts struggle to keep up with this sheer volume of data, making it difficult to identify potential threats. AI excels in handling large datasets, quickly analyzing and correlating data from multiple sources to detect patterns and anomalies that may indicate a security threat. This capability enables organizations to sift through vast amounts of data and pinpoint potential issues with greater accuracy and efficiency.

REAL-TIME THREAT DETECTION AND RESPONSE

In today's fast-paced digital environment, the ability to detect and respond to threats in real-time is crucial. Cyber attackers can exploit vulnerabilities and cause significant damage within minutes. AI-driven security solutions can continuously monitor network traffic and system activities, identifying threats as they occur. Machine learning algorithms can analyze data in real-time, flagging suspicious activities and triggering automated responses to mitigate threats before they escalate. This proactive approach helps organizations minimize the impact of cyberattacks and maintain the integrity of their systems and data.

ADAPTIVE LEARNING AND EVOLUTION

Cyber threats are constantly evolving, with attackers developing new techniques to bypass traditional security measures. AI systems are capable of adaptive learning, meaning they can continuously improve their understanding of threats by analyzing new data and incorporating feedback. Machine learning models can be trained on a variety of datasets, including historical attack data, threat intelligence feeds, and simulated attack scenarios. As AI systems learn from these datasets, they become better equipped to identify emerging threats and adapt to changing attack vectors. This adaptability ensures that AI-driven security solutions remain effective even as the threat landscape evolves.

REDUCING FALSE POSITIVES AND FALSE NEGATIVES

One of the challenges faced by traditional security systems is the high rate of false positives and false negatives. False positives occur when legitimate activities are incorrectly flagged as threats, leading to unnecessary

12

investigations and resource allocation. False negatives, on the other hand, are actual threats that go undetected, leaving the organization vulnerable to attacks. AI can significantly reduce both false positives and false negatives by analyzing data with greater precision and context-awareness. Machine learning algorithms can differentiate between normal and abnormal behaviour, reducing the likelihood of false alerts and ensuring that genuine threats are promptly identified and addressed.

ENHANCING THREAT INTELLIGENCE

AI enhances threat intelligence by aggregating and analyzing data from various sources, including threat intelligence feeds, dark web monitoring, and open-source intelligence. By leveraging natural language processing (NLP) and machine learning, AI systems can identify relevant information about emerging threats, threat actors, and attack methods. This enriched threat intelligence enables organizations to stay informed about the latest developments in the cybersecurity landscape and take proactive measures to protect their systems. AI-driven threat intelligence platforms can also provide real-time alerts and recommendations, helping security teams prioritize their efforts and respond to threats more effectively.

AUGMENTING HUMAN EXPERTISE

While AI is transforming the landscape of cybersecurity, it is important to recognize that it is not a replacement for human expertise. Rather, AI serves as a force multiplier for security teams, augmenting their capabilities and allowing them to work more efficiently and effectively. AI can handle routine tasks and large-scale data analysis, freeing up security professionals to focus on more complex and strategic activities. By leveraging AI, security teams can improve their decision-making processes, enhance their threat detection and response capabilities, and ultimately strengthen their organization's overall security posture.

PROACTIVE SECURITY MEASURES

Traditional cybersecurity measures are often reactive, responding to threats after they have been detected. AI enables a more proactive approach to security by predicting and preventing potential threats before they can cause harm. Predictive analytics, powered by machine learning, can identify vulnerabilities and potential attack vectors, allowing organizations to address them proactively. Additionally, AI can simulate potential attack scenarios and test the effectiveness of existing security measures, providing valuable insights for improving defenses.

SCALABILITY AND EFFICIENCY

As organizations grow and their IT environments become more complex, scalability becomes a critical factor in maintaining effective cybersecurity. AI-driven solutions are inherently scalable, capable of handling increasing amounts of data and adapting to expanding networks and systems. This scalability ensures that organizations can maintain robust security measures as they grow, without compromising on efficiency or effectiveness. AI also improves operational efficiency by automating repetitive tasks, reducing the workload on security teams, and enabling faster response times to incidents.

INTEGRATION WITH EXISTING SYSTEMS

AI can be seamlessly integrated with existing cybersecurity tools and systems, enhancing their capabilities and providing a unified approach to threat detection and response. For example, AI-driven analytics can be integrated with SIEM systems to improve event correlation and anomaly detection. AI-powered threat intelligence platforms can work alongside existing security tools to provide comprehensive insights and recommendations. This integration ensures that organizations can leverage the power of AI without disrupting their existing security infrastructure.

AI TECHNOLOGIES IN CYBERSECURITY

MACHINE LEARNING (ML)

Machine Learning (ML) is a subset of artificial intelligence that involves training algorithms to identify patterns in data and make predictions or decisions based on that data. In the context of cybersecurity, ML is used to detect anomalies, predict potential threats, and automate responses to attacks. By leveraging large datasets, ML algorithms can learn from historical data and improve their accuracy over time.

APPLICATIONS IN CYBERSECURITY

Machine learning can be applied to various aspects of cybersecurity, including:

- **Intrusion Detection:** Identifying unauthorized access attempts by analyzing network traffic and user behavior.

- **Malware Detection:** Recognizing malicious software by analyzing file attributes and behavior patterns.

- **Phishing Detection:** Detecting phishing attempts by analyzing email content and sender information.

- **User Authentication:** Enhancing authentication mechanisms by analyzing user behavior and identifying anomalies.

- **Threat Intelligence:** Aggregating and analyzing threat data to identify emerging threats and trends.

SUPERVISED LEARNING

Supervised learning involves training models on labeled data, where the outcome or label is known. The model learns to map input data to the correct output by finding patterns in the labeled data. Once trained, the model can make predictions on new, unseen data. Supervised learning is commonly used in classification tasks, such as identifying spam emails or detecting malware.

Examples of supervised learning algorithms:

- **Linear Regression:** Used for predicting continuous values.

- **Logistic Regression:** Used for binary classification tasks.

- **Decision Trees:** Used for both classification and regression tasks.

- **Support Vector Machines (SVM):** Used for classification tasks.

UNSUPERVISED LEARNING

Unsupervised learning involves training models on unlabeled data, where the outcome or label is not known. The model learns to identify patterns and relationships in the data without any prior knowledge of the labels. Unsupervised learning is commonly used in clustering and anomaly detection tasks.

Examples of unsupervised learning algorithms:

- **K-Means Clustering:** Used for partitioning data into distinct clusters.

- **Hierarchical Clustering:** Used for creating a hierarchy of clusters.

- **Principal Component Analysis (PCA):** Used for dimensionality reduction and identifying important features.

- **Autoencoders:** Used for anomaly detection and data compression.

REINFORCEMENT LEARNING

Reinforcement learning involves training models to make decisions by interacting with an environment and receiving feedback in the form of rewards or penalties. The model learns to take actions that maximize cumulative rewards over time. Reinforcement learning is commonly used in dynamic environments, such as adaptive security systems and autonomous threat response.

Examples of reinforcement learning applications:

- **Intrusion Prevention Systems (IPS):** Automatically adjusting security policies based on detected threats.

- **Adaptive Firewalls:** Dynamically updating firewall rules based on network traffic patterns.

- **Autonomous Threat Hunting:** Automatically identifying and mitigating threats in real-time.

CHALLENGES AND CONSIDERATIONS

While machine learning offers significant benefits for cybersecurity, there are also challenges and considerations to keep in mind:

- **Data Quality:** The accuracy of ML models depends on the quality and quantity of the data used for training. Ensuring that data is clean, relevant, and representative of real-world scenarios is crucial.

- **Model Interpretability:** Some ML models, such as deep neural networks, can be complex and difficult to interpret. Ensuring that security analysts can understand and trust the model's decisions is important.

- **Adversarial Attacks:** Attackers may attempt to deceive ML models by introducing adversarial examples that cause the model to make incorrect predictions. Developing robust models that can withstand adversarial attacks is essential.

- **Continuous Learning:** Cyber threats are constantly evolving, and ML models need to be continuously updated with new data to remain effective. Implementing mechanisms for continuous learning and model updates is critical for maintaining security.

By addressing these challenges and leveraging the strengths of machine learning, organizations can significantly enhance their cybersecurity posture and better protect against emerging threats.

DEEP LEARNING (DL)

Deep Learning (DL) is a specialized subset of machine learning that uses neural networks with multiple layers (hence "deep") to model and understand complex patterns in large datasets. These neural networks are designed to mimic the human brain, with interconnected nodes (neurons) that process and transmit information. Deep learning is particularly effective at recognizing intricate patterns and relationships in data, making it an invaluable tool in fields such as image and speech recognition, natural language processing, and cybersecurity.

ARCHITECTURE OF DEEP LEARNING MODELS

Deep learning models, also known as deep neural networks (DNNs), consist of an input layer, multiple hidden layers, and an output layer. Each layer is composed of nodes that process input data and pass the results to the next layer. The layers in between the input and output layers are called hidden layers, and they perform complex transformations on the data. Common types of deep learning architectures include:

- **Convolutional Neural Networks (CNNs):** Primarily used for image and video recognition, CNNs apply convolutional filters to capture spatial features.

- **Recurrent Neural Networks (RNNs):** Suitable for sequential data like time series or text, RNNs use feedback loops to process sequences of data.

- **Long Short-Term Memory Networks (LSTMs):** A type of RNN designed to capture long-term dependencies, making them ideal for tasks such as language modeling and speech recognition.

- **Generative Adversarial Networks (GANs):** Consist of two networks (a generator and a discriminator) that compete against each other to generate realistic synthetic data.

APPLICATIONS OF DEEP LEARNING

INTRUSION DETECTION

Deep learning can significantly enhance intrusion detection systems (IDS) by identifying patterns in network traffic that indicate malicious activity. CNNs and RNNs can analyze large volumes of network data in real-time, detecting anomalies that traditional methods might miss. For example, a deep learning-based IDS can identify unusual patterns in login attempts or data transfers, flagging potential security breaches for further investigation.

MALWARE ANALYSIS

Deep learning is highly effective in analyzing and classifying malware. By training on large datasets of known malware samples, DNNs can learn to recognize the characteristics of malicious code. This allows the model to identify new and unknown malware variants based on their behavior or code structure. Techniques like binary analysis and static and dynamic analysis can be enhanced with deep learning to improve the accuracy and speed of malware detection.

BEHAVIOURAL ANALYSIS

Deep learning models can analyze user behaviour to detect anomalies that may indicate a security threat. By establishing a baseline of normal behavior for each user, the model can identify deviations that suggest compromised accounts or insider threats. For example, if a user's login patterns suddenly change or they start accessing sensitive files they have never accessed before, the system can flag this behavior for further investigation.

PHISHING DETECTION

Phishing attacks often rely on deceptive emails or websites to trick users into providing sensitive information. Deep learning models can analyze the content and structure of emails and web pages to detect phishing attempts. By training on large datasets of phishing and legitimate emails, DNNs can learn to identify subtle indicators of phishing, such as unusual language patterns or suspicious URLs.

FRAUD DETECTION

In the financial sector, deep learning is used to detect fraudulent transactions by analyzing patterns in transaction data. DNNs can identify anomalies that suggest fraud, such as unusually large transactions or transactions that deviate from a user's typical spending behavior. By continuously learning from new data, these models can adapt to emerging fraud techniques and improve their detection capabilities over time.

THREAT INTELLIGENCE

Deep learning can enhance threat intelligence platforms by analyzing vast amounts of threat data and identifying emerging threats. Natural language processing (NLP) techniques can be used to process and analyze text data from threat reports, social media, and dark web forums. By extracting relevant information and identifying patterns, deep learning models can provide valuable insights into the latest threats and vulnerabilities, helping organizations stay ahead of cyber attackers.

CHALLENGES AND CONSIDERATIONS

While deep learning offers significant advantages for cybersecurity, it also comes with challenges:

- **Data Requirements:** Deep learning models require large amounts of labeled data to train effectively. Collecting and labeling this data can be time-consuming and expensive.

- **Computational Resources:** Training deep learning models requires substantial computational power, often necessitating specialized hardware such as GPUs.

- **Interpretability:** Deep learning models can be complex and difficult to interpret. Ensuring that security professionals can understand and trust the model's decisions is crucial for effective implementation.

- **Adversarial Attacks:** Attackers may attempt to deceive deep learning models by introducing adversarial examples that cause the model to make incorrect predictions. Developing robust models that can withstand adversarial attacks is essential.

By addressing these challenges and leveraging the power of deep learning, organizations can significantly enhance their cybersecurity capabilities and better protect against a wide range of threats.

NATURAL LANGUAGE PROCESSING (NLP)

Natural Language Processing (NLP) is a branch of artificial intelligence that focuses on the interaction between computers and human language. NLP techniques enable machines to understand, interpret, and generate human language, making it a powerful tool in cybersecurity. By analyzing text data, NLP can help identify malicious communications, detect phishing attempts, and extract valuable information from threat intelligence reports.

APPLICATIONS IN CYBERSECURITY

NLP is used in various cybersecurity applications, including:

- **Email Filtering:** Detecting spam and phishing emails by analyzing their content and identifying suspicious patterns.

- **Threat Intelligence:** Extracting relevant information from unstructured text data, such as security reports and dark web forums.

- **Chatbot Security:** Ensuring that automated chatbots used in customer service are not exploited for malicious purposes.

- **Sentiment Analysis:** Monitoring social media and other communication channels for potential security threats based on sentiment and content.

NLP TECHNIQUES

TOKENIZATION

Tokenization involves breaking down text into individual words or tokens. This is the first step in most NLP tasks, allowing the text to be analyzed at a granular level. By tokenizing an email, for example, NLP algorithms can examine each word and its context to identify suspicious terms or phrases commonly used in phishing attempts.

Named Entity Recognition (NER)

Named Entity Recognition (NER) involves identifying and classifying entities in text, such as names, dates, and locations. In cybersecurity, NER can be used to extract critical information from threat reports or social media posts, such as the names of malware variants, affected organizations, or geographical locations of attacks.

SENTIMENT ANALYSIS

Sentiment analysis determines the sentiment or emotional tone of a text, such as positive, negative, or neutral. In cybersecurity, sentiment analysis can be used to monitor social media and other communication channels for potential threats. For example, a sudden spike in negative sentiment towards a particular organization could indicate an impending cyberattack.

TEXT CLASSIFICATION

Text classification involves categorizing text into predefined categories. In cybersecurity, this can be used to classify emails as spam or legitimate, or to categorize threat intelligence reports based on the type of threat (e.g., malware, phishing, or DDoS attacks). Machine learning algorithms, such as support vector machines (SVM) or deep learning models, are commonly used for text classification tasks.

LANGUAGE MODELING

Language modeling involves predicting the next word or sequence of words in a text. This technique is used in various NLP applications, such as autocomplete and text generation. In cybersecurity, language modeling can be used to identify and block malicious text inputs that deviate from normal language patterns.

ANOMALY DETECTION

Anomaly detection involves identifying patterns in data that do not conform to expected behavior. In cybersecurity, anomaly detection is used to spot unusual activities that may indicate a security breach or malicious behavior. This can include detecting abnormal login attempts, unusual data transfers, or irregular user activities.

APPLICATIONS IN CYBERSECURITY

- **Network Monitoring:** Analyzing network traffic to detect anomalies that may indicate a cyberattack, such as unusual data spikes or communication with known malicious IP addresses.

24

- **User Behaviour Analytics (UBA):** Monitoring user activities to detect deviations from normal behavior, which could indicate insider threats or compromised accounts.

- **Endpoint Security:** Detecting unusual activities on endpoints, such as the execution of unknown processes or unexpected changes to system files.

- **Fraud Detection:** Identifying fraudulent transactions by analyzing patterns and anomalies in transaction data.

EXAMPLE: ANOMALY DETECTION IN ACTION

CASE STUDY: DETECTING UNAUTHORIZED ACCESS ATTEMPTS

Company X implemented an anomaly detection system to monitor user login patterns. The system established a baseline of normal login behaviour for each employee, including typical login times, locations, and devices. One day, the system detected a series of login attempts from an employee's account at unusual times and from an unfamiliar IP address. The anomaly detection system flagged these attempts as suspicious and alerted the security team.

Upon investigation, the security team discovered that the employee's account had been compromised by an attacker who had obtained their login credentials through a phishing email. The timely detection and response prevented the attacker from accessing sensitive data and causing further damage. This example demonstrates how anomaly detection can effectively identify and mitigate potential security threats by recognizing deviations from normal behaviour.

By leveraging NLP and anomaly detection techniques, organizations can significantly enhance their cybersecurity posture and better protect against a wide range of threats. These technologies provide valuable insights into potential security issues, enabling proactive measures to prevent and mitigate cyberattacks.

INTRODUCTION TO OCR

Optical Character Recognition (OCR) is a technology that converts different types of documents, such as scanned paper documents, PDF files, or images captured by a digital camera, into editable and searchable data. OCR technology enables machines to read printed or handwritten text by recognizing the characters and converting them into machine-readable code. This technology plays a crucial role in automating data entry processes, extracting information from documents, and enhancing data accessibility.

APPLICATIONS IN CYBERSECURITY

In cybersecurity, OCR is used to analyze and extract information from various text-based sources, such as scanned documents, images, and PDFs. This capability is essential for identifying potential threats hidden within documents, such as embedded malware, phishing attempts, and malicious code.

TECHNICAL DETAILS

ALGORITHMS AND TECHNIQUES

OCR systems use a combination of machine learning algorithms and image processing techniques to recognize and convert text. The main steps involved in OCR processing include:

- **Image Preprocessing:** Enhancing the quality of the input image by removing noise, correcting distortions, and improving contrast.

- **Segmentation:** Dividing the image into smaller regions, such as lines, words, and characters, to facilitate text recognition.

- **Feature Extraction:** Identifying distinctive features of each character, such as edges, corners, and strokes, to aid in recognition.

- **Classification:** Comparing the extracted features with a database of known characters using machine learning models to identify the correct characters.

- **Post-Processing:** Refining the recognized text by correcting errors, identifying context-specific patterns, and improving accuracy.

ADVANCEMENTS IN OCR

Recent advancements in OCR technology have significantly improved its accuracy and efficiency. Deep learning models, such as convolutional neural networks (CNNs) and recurrent neural networks (RNNs), have enhanced the ability of OCR systems to recognize complex and distorted text. Additionally, the integration of natural language processing (NLP) techniques has enabled OCR systems to understand the context and meaning of the extracted text, further improving accuracy.

EXTENDED USE CASES

FINANCIAL SECTOR

In the financial sector, OCR technology is used to automate the processing of invoices, receipts, and other financial documents. By extracting and validating data from these documents, OCR helps reduce manual data entry errors, streamline workflows, and ensure compliance with regulatory requirements. Additionally, OCR can be used to detect fraudulent activities by analyzing scanned images of checks, identifying forgeries, and verifying signatures.

HEALTHCARE INDUSTRY

OCR technology is widely used in the healthcare industry to digitize patient records, medical forms, and prescription labels. By converting handwritten and printed text into electronic data, OCR improves data accessibility, enhances patient care, and ensures compliance with health information privacy regulations. Additionally, OCR can be used to analyze medical images, such as X-rays and MRIs, to extract relevant information for diagnostic purposes.

LEGAL SECTOR

In the legal sector, OCR technology is used to digitize and organize large volumes of legal documents, such as contracts, case files, and court records. By converting these documents into searchable and editable formats, OCR enhances data retrieval, improves document management, and facilitates legal research. Additionally, OCR can be used to extract key information from legal documents for analysis and decision-making.

EDUCATION SECTOR

In the education sector, OCR technology is used to digitize textbooks, exam papers, and student records. By converting printed and handwritten text into electronic data, OCR improves data accessibility, enhances the learning experience, and streamlines administrative processes. Additionally, OCR can be used to analyze handwritten essays and assignments, providing automated grading and feedback to students.

FUTURE DIRECTIONS

ENHANCED ACCURACY AND SPEED

Ongoing research and development in OCR technology aim to further improve its accuracy and speed. Advances in deep learning and artificial intelligence are expected to enhance the ability of OCR systems to recognize complex text, handle diverse languages, and process large volumes of data more efficiently. Additionally, the integration of advanced image processing techniques is expected to improve the quality of input images, reducing the need for manual preprocessing.

INTEGRATION WITH OTHER TECHNOLOGIES

The integration of OCR technology with other emerging technologies, such as blockchain and the Internet of Things (IoT), is expected to create new opportunities for enhanced security and data management. For example,

OCR can be used to extract and validate data from IoT devices, ensuring the accuracy and integrity of the collected information. Additionally, the integration of OCR with blockchain can enhance data traceability and security, providing a tamper-proof record of document processing activities.

APPLICATIONS IN CYBERSECURITY

In cybersecurity, future advancements in OCR technology are expected to enhance its ability to detect and prevent document-based threats. By leveraging advanced machine learning algorithms and threat intelligence, OCR systems can identify malicious content hidden within documents, such as embedded malware, phishing attempts, and malicious code. Additionally, OCR can be used to automate the analysis of security reports, extracting relevant information and providing actionable insights to security teams.

OCR technology has revolutionized the way organizations process and manage text-based data. Its applications in various sectors, including finance, healthcare, legal, and education, have enhanced data accessibility, improved efficiency, and ensured compliance with regulatory requirements. As OCR technology continues to evolve, its integration with other emerging technologies and advancements in artificial intelligence are expected to create new opportunities for enhanced security, accuracy, and efficiency. By leveraging the power of OCR, organizations can unlock the full potential of their data, enhancing their ability to detect and prevent threats and improve overall operational efficiency.

VISUAL AI TECHNOLOGIES

INTRODUCTION TO VISUAL AI

Visual AI involves the application of artificial intelligence techniques to analyze visual data, such as images and videos. By leveraging machine learning and deep learning algorithms, Visual AI can process and interpret visual information, enabling a wide range of applications in various industries. In cybersecurity, Visual AI is used to monitor and analyze surveillance footage, detect suspicious behavior, and ensure secure access control.

APPLICATIONS IN CYBERSECURITY

Visual AI enhances cybersecurity by providing real-time monitoring and analysis of visual data, helping organizations detect and respond to potential threats. Some common applications include:

- **Surveillance Monitoring:** Analyzing CCTV footage to detect unauthorized access or suspicious behaviour.

- **Facial Recognition:** Identifying individuals based on facial features for secure access control.

- **Object Detection:** Identifying objects in images or videos, such as weapons or suspicious packages.

- **Anomaly Detection:** Detecting unusual activities or patterns in visual data that may indicate a security threat.

ADVANCED TECHNIQUES

CONVOLUTIONAL NEURAL NETWORKS (CNNS)

Convolutional Neural Networks (CNNs) are a class of deep learning models specifically designed for processing visual data. CNNs use convolutional layers to extract features from images, such as edges, textures, and shapes, which are then used to classify or recognize objects. CNNs are highly effective in image recognition and object detection tasks, making them a key component of Visual AI systems.

GENERATIVE ADVERSARIAL NETWORKS (GANS)

Generative Adversarial Networks (GANs) consist of two neural networks—a generator and a discriminator—that compete against each other. The generator creates synthetic images, while the discriminator evaluates their authenticity. This competition improves the quality of the generated images over time. GANs are used in various applications, including data augmentation, where they generate realistic images to enhance the training dataset, and in security training, where they simulate potential attack scenarios.

RECURRENT NEURAL NETWORKS (RNNS)

Recurrent Neural Networks (RNNs) are designed to handle sequential data, making them suitable for analyzing video streams. RNNs can capture temporal dependencies, allowing them to understand the sequence of events in a video. This capability is particularly useful in applications such as behaviour analysis, where understanding the progression of actions is crucial for detecting anomalies.

PRIVACY AND ETHICAL CONSIDERATIONS

PRIVACY CONCERNS

The use of Visual AI in surveillance and facial recognition raises significant privacy concerns. Continuous monitoring of individuals can infringe on their privacy rights, leading to potential misuse or abuse of the collected data. To address these concerns, organizations must implement robust data protection measures, such as anonymizing data, encrypting sensitive information, and ensuring compliance with privacy regulations.

ETHICAL CONSIDERATIONS

The deployment of Visual AI systems must be guided by ethical principles to ensure their responsible use. Ethical considerations include:

- **Transparency:** Ensuring that the use of Visual AI is transparent and that individuals are informed about how their data is being collected and used.

- **Bias Mitigation:** Addressing biases in Visual AI models to prevent discrimination based on race, gender, or other attributes.

- **Accountability:** Establishing clear accountability mechanisms to address any misuse or errors in Visual AI systems.

- **Consent:** Obtaining explicit consent from individuals before collecting and using their visual data.

REGULATORY COMPLIANCE

Organizations must adhere to relevant regulations and standards when implementing Visual AI systems. Regulations such as the General Data Protection Regulation (GDPR) in Europe and the California Consumer Privacy Act (CCPA) in the United States provide guidelines for data protection and privacy. Compliance with these regulations is essential to ensure the lawful and ethical use of Visual AI technologies.

FUTURE DIRECTIONS

ADVANCEMENTS IN IMAGE AND VIDEO PROCESSING

Future advancements in image and video processing are expected to enhance the capabilities of Visual AI systems. Techniques such as super-resolution imaging, which improves the quality of low-resolution images, and real-time video analysis, which enables instantaneous threat detection, are areas of active research. These advancements will improve the accuracy and efficiency of Visual AI systems, making them more effective in cybersecurity applications.

INTEGRATION WITH OTHER AI TECHNOLOGIES

The integration of Visual AI with other AI technologies, such as natural language processing (NLP) and machine learning, will create more comprehensive security solutions. For example, combining Visual AI with NLP can enhance the analysis of multimedia content, allowing for the detection of threats in both visual and textual data. This integration will provide organizations with a more holistic view of potential security risks.

IMPROVED HARDWARE FOR VISUAL AI

Advancements in hardware, such as more powerful GPUs and specialized AI chips, will enable faster and more efficient processing of visual data. These improvements will allow Visual AI systems to analyze larger volumes of data in real-time, enhancing their ability to detect and respond to threats promptly. Additionally, edge computing technologies, which process data closer to its source, will reduce latency and improve the performance of Visual AI systems in real-time applications.

EXPANDED USE CASES

The future will see an expansion of Visual AI use cases beyond traditional security applications. For instance, Visual AI can be used in smart cities to enhance public safety by monitoring traffic and detecting accidents. In retail, Visual AI can analyze customer behaviour to improve store layouts and optimize inventory management. These expanded use cases will drive further innovation and adoption of Visual AI technologies.

Visual AI technologies are transforming the way organizations monitor and analyze visual data, providing enhanced security and operational efficiency. By leveraging advanced techniques such as CNNs, GANs, and RNNs, Visual AI systems can detect and respond to threats in real-time. However, the implementation of Visual AI must be guided by ethical principles and regulatory compliance to address privacy concerns and ensure responsible use. As advancements in image and video processing, hardware, and integration with other AI technologies continue, Visual AI will play an increasingly critical role in various industries, driving innovation and improving security outcomes.

CASE STUDIES

INTRODUCTION

Case studies provide valuable insights into the practical applications of AI in cybersecurity. By examining real-world examples, we can understand the challenges, solutions, and outcomes of implementing AI technologies. These case studies highlight the effectiveness of AI in addressing specific cybersecurity issues and offer lessons learned that can be applied in other contexts.

IN-DEPTH ANALYSIS

Each case study includes a detailed analysis of the challenges faced, the solutions implemented, and the outcomes achieved. This analysis helps to highlight the effectiveness of AI in addressing specific cybersecurity issues and provides valuable lessons for future implementations.

CASE STUDY 1: FINANCIAL SECTOR

CHALLENGES

The financial sector faces a wide range of fraud types, including credit card fraud, identity theft, and insider trading. The complexity of transaction patterns and the need to comply with stringent regulatory requirements add to the challenge. Financial institutions must protect sensitive customer information and ensure the integrity of financial transactions, all while maintaining compliance with industry standards such as PCI DSS.

SOLUTIONS IMPLEMENTED

To address these challenges, the financial institution implemented machine learning algorithms, including decision trees and neural networks, to analyze transaction patterns and detect anomalies. These algorithms were trained on historical transaction data, allowing them to identify patterns indicative of fraudulent activity. Data sources included transaction logs, customer profiles, and external fraud databases. The AI system was integrated with existing fraud detection systems to provide real-time alerts.

The solution also included:

- **Behavioural Analytics:** Monitoring customer behaviour to detect deviations from typical activity.

- **Real-Time Monitoring:** Continuously analyzing transaction data to identify and flag suspicious activities.

- **Risk Scoring:** Assigning risk scores to transactions based on their likelihood of being fraudulent, allowing for prioritized investigations.

OUTCOMES

The implementation of AI-driven fraud detection resulted in a 40% reduction in fraudulent transactions and cost savings of millions of dollars. The detection rates improved by 30%, significantly enhancing the institution's ability to prevent fraud. Additionally, the AI system reduced the number of false positives, minimizing unnecessary investigations and improving operational efficiency. The financial institution also reported improved customer satisfaction due to quicker response times and better protection of customer data.

KEY TAKEAWAYS

- **Effective Use of Machine Learning:** Leveraging machine learning algorithms to analyze large volumes of transaction data can significantly enhance fraud detection capabilities.

- **Integration with Existing Systems:** Integrating AI solutions with existing fraud detection systems ensures seamless operation and maximizes the benefits of both technologies.

- **Continuous Improvement:** Regular updates and retraining of machine learning models are essential to maintain their effectiveness against evolving fraud tactics.

CASE STUDY 2: HEALTHCARE SECTOR

CHALLENGES

Healthcare providers must protect sensitive patient data while ensuring real-time access for authorized personnel. Data privacy concerns, the diversity of data formats, and the need for continuous monitoring present significant challenges. Additionally, healthcare organizations must comply with regulations such as the Health Insurance Portability and Accountability Act (HIPAA).

SOLUTIONS IMPLEMENTED

The healthcare provider implemented AI models, including anomaly detection algorithms and access pattern analysis, to monitor access logs. The AI system was designed to detect unauthorized access attempts and ensure compliance with healthcare regulations. Data sources included electronic health records (EHRs), access logs, and user activity data. The AI-driven solution provided real-time monitoring and alerts, enabling quick response to potential breaches.

The solution also included:

- **User Behaviour Analytics:** Monitoring user activities to detect anomalies that may indicate insider threats or compromised accounts.

- **Automated Compliance Checks:** Ensuring continuous compliance with HIPAA by automatically monitoring access and data handling practices.

- **Data Encryption:** Implementing advanced encryption techniques to protect patient data both at rest and in transit.

OUTCOMES

The AI system enhanced patient data security by reducing unauthorized access attempts by 50%. The implementation led to a significant improvement in data protection, ensuring that sensitive information remained secure while maintaining accessibility for authorized personnel. Additionally, the healthcare provider reported increased compliance with HIPAA regulations and reduced risk of data breaches. The AI-driven solution also improved operational efficiency by automating routine monitoring tasks.

KEY TAKEAWAYS

- **Real-Time Monitoring:** Continuous monitoring of access logs and user activities is crucial for detecting and preventing unauthorized access.

- **Automated Compliance:** AI can help healthcare providers maintain compliance with regulatory requirements by automating compliance checks and reporting.

- **Enhanced Data Protection:** Implementing AI-driven security measures, such as anomaly detection and data encryption, can significantly enhance the protection of sensitive patient data.

CASE STUDY 3: GOVERNMENT SECTOR

CHALLENGES

Government agencies face a wide range of cyber threats, including espionage, data breaches, and denial-of-service attacks. The need to protect classified information and critical infrastructure adds to the complexity. Additionally, government agencies must comply with stringent security standards and regulations.

SOLUTIONS IMPLEMENTED

The government agency implemented AI-driven security solutions, including threat intelligence platforms and predictive analytics, to enhance their cybersecurity posture. The AI system aggregated data from multiple sources, including threat intelligence feeds, social media, and dark web monitoring, to identify emerging threats. Predictive analytics were used to forecast potential attack vectors and prioritize security measures.

The solution also included:

- **Advanced Threat Intelligence:** Leveraging AI to analyze and correlate data from various sources to provide actionable insights.

- **Predictive Analytics:** Using machine learning models to predict potential threats and vulnerabilities based on historical data and current trends.

- **Automated Incident Response:** Implementing AI-driven response mechanisms to quickly mitigate detected threats and minimize damage.

OUTCOMES

The AI-driven security solution significantly enhanced the government's ability to detect and respond to cyber threats. The predictive analytics model accurately forecasted potential attack vectors, allowing the agency to proactively strengthen their defences. The implementation resulted in a 60% reduction in successful cyberattacks and improved the agency's overall security posture. Additionally, the automated incident response capabilities reduced the time to contain and mitigate threats, minimizing the impact of cyber incidents.

KEY TAKEAWAYS

- **Proactive Threat Detection:** Predictive analytics enable government agencies to anticipate and prepare for potential cyber threats.

- **Comprehensive Threat Intelligence:** Aggregating and analyzing data from multiple sources provides a more holistic view of the threat landscape.

- **Rapid Incident Response:** AI-driven incident response mechanisms can significantly reduce the time to contain and mitigate threats, minimizing their impact.

By examining these case studies, organizations can gain valuable insights into the practical applications of AI in cybersecurity and learn from the experiences of others in implementing and leveraging AI-driven solutions to enhance their security posture.

IMPLEMENTATION STRATEGIES

Implementing AI in cybersecurity requires a strategic approach to ensure success. This involves careful planning, selecting the right technologies, and ensuring seamless integration with existing systems. In this section, we outline the key steps and best practices for implementing AI-driven cybersecurity solutions.

IMPLEMENTATION

STEP 1: ASSESSING THE CURRENT SECURITY POSTURE

Before implementing AI, organizations need to assess their current security posture. This involves identifying existing vulnerabilities, understanding the current threat landscape, and evaluating the effectiveness of existing security measures. Conducting a thorough risk assessment helps in determining the specific areas where AI can add the most value.

Key Activities:

- Risk Assessment: Conduct a comprehensive risk assessment to identify vulnerabilities and potential threats.

- Gap Analysis: Perform a gap analysis to evaluate the effectiveness of current security measures and identify areas for improvement.

•　　　Resource Evaluation: Assess available resources, including budget, personnel, and technology infrastructure, to support AI implementation.

Clear objectives and requirements are essential for the successful implementation of AI in cybersecurity. Organizations need to define what they aim to achieve with AI, such as improving threat detection, reducing response times, or enhancing overall security posture. Defining specific use cases and success criteria helps in measuring the effectiveness of the AI implementation.

Key Activities:

•　　　**Objective Setting:** Define clear objectives for AI implementation, such as enhanced threat detection or improved incident response.

•　　　**Use Case Identification:** Identify specific use cases where AI can provide the most value, such as anomaly detection or automated threat intelligence.

•　　　**Success Criteria:** Establish measurable success criteria to evaluate the effectiveness of AI implementation, such as reduced false positives or faster threat response times.

Choosing the right AI technologies is critical for achieving desired outcomes. This involves evaluating various AI techniques, such as machine learning, deep learning, and natural language processing, and selecting the ones that best meet the organization's objectives and requirements. Collaborating with AI experts and vendors can help in making informed decisions.

Key Activities:

- **Technology Evaluation:** Evaluate different AI technologies and solutions based on their capabilities, scalability, and compatibility with existing systems.

- **Vendor Selection:** Identify and engage with reputable AI vendors and solution providers who can support the implementation process.

- **Proof of Concept (PoC):** Conduct a PoC to test the selected AI technologies in a controlled environment and validate their effectiveness.

STEP 4: INTEGRATING AI WITH EXISTING SECURITY SYSTEMS

AI technologies need to be seamlessly integrated with existing security systems to maximize their effectiveness. This involves ensuring compatibility with existing tools and platforms, setting up data pipelines for continuous data flow, and establishing communication channels for real-time alerts and notifications. Proper integration ensures that AI-driven insights can be effectively acted upon.

Key Activities:

- **System Integration:** Ensure seamless integration of AI technologies with existing security infrastructure, such as SIEM systems, firewalls, and endpoint protection tools.

- **Data Management:** Set up robust data pipelines to ensure continuous data flow for AI analysis and decision-making.

- **Alert Mechanisms:** Establish real-time alert mechanisms to enable quick response to identified threats.

STEP 5: TRAINING AND TESTING AI MODELS

Training AI models with relevant data is crucial for their accuracy and effectiveness. This involves collecting and preprocessing data, selecting appropriate training algorithms, and continuously refining the models based on feedback and performance metrics. Rigorous testing in controlled environments helps in identifying and addressing potential issues before deployment.

Key Activities:

- **Data Collection:** Gather relevant data from various sources, such as network logs, threat intelligence feeds, and user activity logs, for training AI models.

- **Model Training:** Train AI models using supervised, unsupervised, or reinforcement learning techniques, depending on the use case.

- **Performance Evaluation:** Continuously evaluate the performance of AI models using metrics such as accuracy, precision, and recall, and refine the models based on feedback.

STEP 6: MONITORING AND CONTINUOUS IMPROVEMENT

Once AI technologies are deployed, continuous monitoring is essential to ensure they are functioning as expected. This involves tracking performance metrics, analyzing false positives and false negatives, and making necessary adjustments to improve accuracy. Regular updates and maintenance help in keeping the AI systems up to date with evolving threats.

Key Activities:

- **Performance Monitoring:** Continuously monitor the performance of AI systems and track key metrics to ensure they are functioning as expected.

- **Feedback Loop:** Establish a feedback loop to gather insights from security analysts and users and use this feedback to improve AI models.

- **Regular Updates:** Regularly update AI models and systems to ensure they remain effective against emerging threats and vulnerabilities.

BEST PRACTICES FOR SUCCESSFUL IMPLEMENTATION

- Collaborate with AI experts and cybersecurity professionals to leverage their expertise.

- Ensure data quality and relevance for training AI models.

- Establish clear communication channels for sharing AI-driven insights.

- Continuously monitor and update AI systems to adapt to new threats.

- Evaluate the effectiveness of AI implementation through regular assessments and audits.

CHALLENGES AND SOLUTIONS

Implementing AI in cybersecurity comes with its own set of challenges, such as data privacy concerns, integration complexities, and the need for specialized skills. Addressing these challenges requires a strategic approach and collaboration with stakeholders across the organization. By proactively identifying and mitigating potential issues, organizations can ensure the successful implementation of AI-driven cybersecurity solutions.

KEY CHALLENGES:

- **Data Privacy:** Ensuring the privacy and security of data used for training AI models.

- **Integration Complexities:** Seamlessly integrating AI technologies with existing security systems and infrastructure.

- **Specialized Skills:** Acquiring and developing the necessary skills and expertise to implement and manage AI-driven solutions.

SOLUTIONS:

- **Privacy Measures:** Implement robust data privacy measures, such as anonymization and encryption, to protect sensitive data.

- **Integration Planning:** Develop a comprehensive integration plan that includes compatibility checks, testing, and validation.

- **Training Programs:** Invest in training programs and professional development to build the necessary skills and expertise within the organization.

By following these implementation steps and best practices, organizations can effectively leverage AI to enhance their cybersecurity posture, improve threat detection and response, and ensure a robust and resilient security framework.

The field of AI in cybersecurity is continuously evolving, with new trends and technologies emerging at a rapid pace. Staying ahead of these trends is crucial for organizations to maintain a robust security posture. In this section, we explore some of the key future trends in AI-driven cybersecurity and their potential impact on the industry.

EMERGING AI TECHNOLOGIES

QUANTUM COMPUTING

Quantum computing promises to revolutionize data processing and encryption techniques, providing unprecedented levels of security. Quantum computers can solve complex problems much faster than classical computers, enabling them to break traditional encryption methods. This potential poses a significant challenge for cybersecurity, as new quantum-resistant encryption algorithms will need to be developed. On the other hand, quantum computing can enhance AI capabilities, improving threat detection and response times.

FEDERATED LEARNING

Federated learning enables collaborative learning across multiple organizations without sharing sensitive data. This approach allows AI models to be trained on decentralized data, enhancing privacy and security. In cybersecurity, federated learning can improve threat intelligence by aggregating insights from different organizations while maintaining data confidentiality. This collaborative approach helps in creating more robust and comprehensive security solutions.

EXPLAINABLE AI

As AI systems become more complex, the need for explainable AI grows. Explainable AI involves developing models that can provide clear and understandable explanations for their decisions, improving transparency and trust. In cybersecurity, explainable AI can help security analysts understand the reasoning behind AI-driven alerts and recommendations, making it easier to interpret and act on them. This transparency is crucial for ensuring that AI systems are used responsibly and effectively.

INCREASED FOCUS ON PRIVACY AND ETHICS

DATA PRIVACY REGULATIONS

As AI technologies become more prevalent in cybersecurity, there is a growing focus on privacy and ethical considerations. Organizations must ensure that their AI-driven security measures comply with data protection regulations such as the General Data Protection Regulation (GDPR) and the California Consumer Privacy Act (CCPA). This involves implementing robust data anonymization techniques, ensuring transparency in AI decision-making, and addressing potential biases in AI models.

ETHICAL AI PRACTICES

Adopting ethical AI practices is essential for building trust and ensuring the responsible use of AI in cybersecurity. This includes:

- **Bias Mitigation:** Ensuring that AI models are free from biases that could lead to unfair or discriminatory outcomes.

- **Transparency:** Providing clear and understandable explanations for AI-driven decisions and actions.

- **Accountability:** Establishing mechanisms to hold organizations accountable for the ethical use of AI.

- **User Consent:** Obtaining explicit consent from individuals before using their data for AI-driven security measures.

AI-DRIVEN THREAT INTELLIGENCE

REAL-TIME INSIGHTS

AI-driven threat intelligence is expected to play a crucial role in the future of cybersecurity. By leveraging advanced data analytics and machine learning, AI can provide real-time insights into emerging threats and vulnerabilities. This enables organizations to proactively address potential risks and enhance their overall security posture. AI-driven threat intelligence platforms can aggregate data from various sources, including threat feeds, social media, and dark web monitoring, to provide comprehensive and up-to-date information on the latest threats.

INTEGRATION WITH SECURITY OPERATIONS

Integrating AI-driven threat intelligence with security operations centers (SOCs) can significantly enhance threat detection and response capabilities. AI can automate the analysis of threat data, reducing the time and effort required by security analysts. By providing real-time alerts and recommendations, AI-driven threat intelligence helps SOCs prioritize and address the most critical threats, improving overall efficiency and effectiveness.

BLOCKCHAIN

The integration of AI with blockchain technology can enhance data integrity and traceability. Blockchain provides a decentralized and tamper-proof record of transactions, making it ideal for securing sensitive data and ensuring transparency. By combining AI with blockchain, organizations can create more secure and trustworthy systems for managing and protecting data. For example, AI-driven threat detection systems can use blockchain to verify the authenticity of data and ensure that it has not been tampered with.

INTERNET OF THINGS (IOT)

The proliferation of IoT devices presents new challenges and opportunities for cybersecurity. AI-powered IoT security solutions can provide real-time monitoring and threat detection for connected devices. By analyzing data from IoT devices, AI can identify unusual patterns and behaviors that may indicate a security threat. This proactive approach helps in preventing attacks on IoT networks and ensuring the security of connected devices.

AUTONOMOUS CYBERSECURITY SYSTEMS

The future of cybersecurity is likely to see the rise of autonomous security systems that can operate with minimal human intervention. These systems will leverage AI and machine learning to detect and respond to threats in real-time, reducing the burden on security teams and improving overall efficiency. Autonomous cybersecurity systems have the potential to significantly enhance threat detection and response times, providing organizations with a more robust security posture.

EVOLVING THREAT LANDSCAPE

As cyber threats continue to evolve, AI-driven cybersecurity solutions need to continuously learn and adapt to stay effective. This involves implementing continuous learning frameworks that enable AI models to update their knowledge based on new data and emerging threats. By leveraging continuous learning, organizations can ensure that their AI-driven security measures remain relevant and effective in the face of evolving cyber threats.

PROACTIVE DEFENCE

Continuous learning and adaptation also enable organizations to adopt a proactive defence strategy. By anticipating and preparing for potential threats, organizations can take pre-emptive measures to strengthen their defences and mitigate risks. AI-driven solutions can simulate attack scenarios, identify vulnerabilities, and recommend proactive measures to enhance security.

The future of AI in cybersecurity is full of exciting possibilities and opportunities. By staying ahead of emerging trends and technologies, organizations can leverage AI to enhance their security measures and stay protected against evolving threats. As AI continues to evolve, it will play an increasingly critical role in shaping the future of cybersecurity, providing organizations with the tools and capabilities they need to stay ahead of the curve. Embracing these advancements and integrating AI-driven solutions into their cybersecurity strategies will be essential for maintaining a robust and resilient security posture in the digital age.

CONCLUSION

THE FUTURE OF AI IN CYBERSECURITY

The integration of AI into cybersecurity is not just a trend; it is a necessity. As cyber threats continue to evolve in complexity and scale, traditional security measures are no longer sufficient. AI technologies, with their ability to analyze vast amounts of data, detect patterns, and respond to threats in real-time, offer a powerful solution to these challenges. By leveraging AI, organizations can enhance their threat detection and response capabilities, improve their overall security posture, and stay ahead of potential threats.

KEY TAKEAWAYS

- **AI Technologies in Cybersecurity:** AI technologies, including machine learning, deep learning, and natural language processing, are revolutionizing threat detection and response in cybersecurity. These technologies enable security systems to analyze vast amounts of data, identify patterns, and detect anomalies with unprecedented accuracy and speed.

- **OCR and Visual AI:** OCR and Visual AI are playing a crucial role in detecting document-based attacks and monitoring visual data for suspicious activities. These technologies enhance data extraction, analysis, and real-time monitoring, providing additional layers of security.

- **Real-World Case Studies:** Case studies from various industries, including finance, healthcare, and government, demonstrate the effectiveness of AI-driven cybersecurity solutions. These examples highlight the practical applications of AI in addressing specific cybersecurity challenges and offer valuable lessons for future implementations.

- **Implementation Strategies:** Successful implementation of AI in cybersecurity requires a strategic approach, including assessing the current security posture, defining objectives, selecting the right technologies, and ensuring seamless integration with existing systems. Continuous monitoring and improvement are essential to maintain the effectiveness of AI-driven security measures.

- **Emerging Trends:** Emerging trends, such as quantum computing, federated learning, explainable AI, and autonomous cybersecurity systems, are shaping the future of AI in cybersecurity. Staying ahead of these trends and integrating them into cybersecurity strategies will be crucial for organizations to maintain a robust security posture.

FINAL THOUGHTS

The journey of integrating AI into cybersecurity is an ongoing process that requires continuous learning, adaptation, and collaboration. Organizations must stay informed about the latest advancements in AI technologies, understand the evolving threat landscape, and proactively update their security measures to stay protected. By embracing AI-driven cybersecurity solutions, organizations can not only enhance their security posture but also build a resilient foundation for the future.

Organizations are encouraged to start exploring and integrating AI technologies into their cybersecurity strategies. This involves not only investing in the right tools and technologies but also fostering a culture of innovation and continuous improvement. By doing so, organizations can better protect their digital assets, ensure compliance with regulatory requirements, and stay ahead of the ever-evolving cyber threats.

ACKNOWLEDGEMENTS

We extend our gratitude to the AI and cybersecurity professionals who have contributed their expertise and insights to this revolutionary industry. Their dedication and commitment to advancing the field of cybersecurity are instrumental in shaping a safer and more secure digital future.

Thank you for taking this journey with us. We hope this book has provided valuable insights and practical guidance on how AI is transforming cybersecurity. Together, we can harness the power of AI to create a safer and more secure digital world.

www.ingramcontent.com/pod-product-compliance
Lightning Source LLC
Chambersburg PA
CBHW070427240526
45472CB00020B/1513